TABLE OF CONTENTS

Resilient was written during a dark time of a Warrior's mental health battle. This book was used as a therapeutic journal as a sense of catharsis during the most pivotal times of her Mental Health Crisis or relationships. *Resilient* will give readers insight into a Warrior's personal struggle with mental health coupled with relationships. The poems are in chronological order to signify her consistent battle of pain that every Warrior faces physically, mentally, and emotionally and the thought pattern that can present itself in various situations. Enjoy the book and take breaks from reading. The material is intense and raw just like the life of a Sickle Cell Warrior.

Attention: Schools and Organizations book bundles are easily accessible on the Golden&Glint website and via invoice.

goldenandglint.com
goldenandglint@gmail.com

Thank you, Nana, for pushing me to continue to excel more than I ever imagined.

Thank you to the doctors and nurses that helped nurse me back to health mentally and physically.

Most importantly I am proud of myself for still being alive and sharing this book with you.

Enjoy!

<u>Dedication</u>

I dedicate this book to those who don't share their mental illness struggle, but still need help.

To those who smile, but are crying on the inside.

To those family's members not knowing how to provide help but still notice their family members' pain.

To those who don't know why they are sad even when everything around them is going great.

Know there is a word for this and its okay to say it.

Depression *(excessive sadness for more than 3-6 months)*

Know that you are not alone.

Know that is it okay to ask for help and express how you are feeling.

I'm Broken

I'm sitting on the bathroom floor, alone,
I feel lonely, hopeless, and abandoned,
All things I've felt before, but it's different
this time
I've been hurt too many times,
I've felt these emotions once too much
and now I'm broken.

Starting to cry, I know for sure
I'm breaking slowly,
How do you fix something that's broken?
How do you pick up the pieces of something
that hurts so much
and not be hurt by it?
They're coming down, like a flood
that a desert has never seen,
when they go into my mouth
they don't taste like water, but bitter salt.

I need help but I know
it will only cause problems for others,
would it even work this time?
Would I even try?

8-26-14
g.r.j

My Thoughts

When I lay down, my thoughts go through my mind
like a cheetah
Little blurred images,
Some are of my childhood,
Others are blank for the future
But why doesn't our brain have a delete button?
I have images that shouldn't be there
You know, those things you wish you never seen
I would never describe them to you because it would
cause immense pain
In the end, our mind is just a landfill for all of our
thoughts

8-27-14
g.r.j

Why is Everything So Complicated

I don't know how to feel
Right now.
I got prayed over today
By my fellow class-members.
I mean,
I even cried,
I felt bad that I sinned,
That I shut God out of my life -
Yet here I am, feeling nothing
Again,
Going on about my day
Like nothing happened an hour ago.
I don't know what to do with myself:
Should I let God in like I always do
But never truly follow through?
Or
Should I just go on
Like he hasn't done everything for me?

I want to rebuild myself but I know I can't
Do it alone and not with the people
I'm surrounded by -
Why is everything so complicated?

9-24-14
g.r.j

Is it Fair?

Is it fair?
That I get to leave school more than 5 times a month?
Go to the hospital more than I spend time at school
I didn't choose my life nobody did but I honestly wish
I did or never wouldn't have been born
I know that sounds kind of harsh but if you were in
my shoes, you would feel the same
It's not fair

9-24-14
g.r.j

My friend has always struggled with life and so have I were we meant to cross paths or drown with each other?

G.R.J

I Think

How do you help someone that is too much like you?
When you're just as unhealthy as them
How are you supposed to bring them up?
My friend has always struggled with life and so have I
Were we meant to cross paths or drown with each
other
All I can do is say I'm sorry and the reaction I get is
the same
We can't help each other
We can only destroy each other
All I want to do is help
But first I need to help myself and now I know that
I think...

9-24-14
g.r.j

God

There are so many signs
I have people in my school that breathe, speak and
love God
I want to be like them one day, I honestly do
I want to walk in his path and catch up to him one day
and be right there with him
Today I got a book that gives me exactly what I need
to do to be there with him
It needs to be my second right hand my new religion
I am declaring this right here in this document for it
to be something I do to make God my everything
Because he created not just me but everything that
surrounds me till this day

9-25-14
g.r.j

What is Bullying?

Is it where you're at the point of waking up an hour
early so you don't have to face the ones you despise?
Is it a simple hateful sentence that comes at you like a
hard rock?
I've been bullied
It's something that happens to everyone
Because it's something that has become human nature
just like sleeping
Right?
But when is too much?
It didn't hurt when it happened
It was how she made me feel afterward
The words came at me like sharp knives with words
attached to them
How could someone I used to be so close to hurt me
like I'm absolutely nothing
I immediately invaded as fast as I could
She made me feel worthless while she held all the
power
The only place I was able to hide was a concealed area
I sat down and instantly felt the flood come out of my
eye sockets.

9-26-14
g.r.j

Then

There's the world then people.
There's love then despair.
Pain then Joy.
Crying then laughter.
Baby then Women.
You have me, an individual, and nothing more to say,
but sorry.

9-30-14
g.r.j

People

I latch onto people
Attachment for me is strong
Like the scent of someone you never want to forget
The warmth of their skin
Taste of someone's lips
Distance makes some relationships strong
However, the desire and feeling of that person never
leaves
Knowing that time is precious &
All you want is to be held and loved

2-25-15
g.r.j

Fighting for Survival

People look at me every day and I know they judge
me.
The way my clothes hang off my body,
How I have so much potential but put forth no effort.
My life is complicated.
Why try when the world has already given up on you?
When you were told it would get better but it never
did.
The world is only as cruel as you let it be.
I feel as if my body is fighting for survival but never
wins.

2-25-15
g.r.j

That's Me

Do you ever just sit with a group of people because
that's what you used to or have been conditioned to
do?
You may not even know anything about them but you
call them your friend
That's me
Friends are hard to come by although you've probably
heard this before
With all the "friends" I have on social media or have
known for years because we went to the same school
I only have one friend
I guess it's better than none
At times I wish
Society would change the idea around how to make
friends
Because then maybe I would have more.

2-26-15
g.r.j

Truly Beautiful

At times I wish I had somebody that was more than a
friend to me
A person that could love me
Just a little bit more than everybody else could
because they truly appreciate me
Everything they see about me is perfect for them
Even when it's a flaw in my eyes
Everything they do is to further their life with me
Every breath I take gives them a reason to live
I want that in life because when you have something
like that it's truly beautiful

2-26-15
g.r.j

Life

People complain about not having that new phone
that just came out or being too skinny.
Being too tall or not having any friends.
People should be less worried about what they don't
have and more grateful for what they do.
I live in pain every day.
There are people who can't talk, see or hear yet we are
still functioning and living in this world just like
everyone else.
The funny thing is, the people who have less tend to
be more grateful than those with more.
They know what it's like to have nothing.
Life is not about what you have or what you do, it's
about the decisions you make and your perspective.

6-29-15
g.r.j

Vital

Maybe if I lay here long enough, they will forget that
I'm alive
They will go on living as if I was never once was there
My body will start to resemble how I feel on the inside
My smile will no longer be a smile
My hair will eventually start to fall out
Bruises will form scars that won't fade and every pill I
take just eats my stomach from within
It would be easier to die knowing that I never meant
anything to anyone that me waking up every day
wasn't vital

11-22-15
g.r.j

Break

I feel as if my body will break with every step
I take,
My brain will explode with every pound
It makes
And every pill I take slowly makes me
Fade away,
This endless cycle is how my body works,
Constantly fighting against itself
And for what?

One day it will stop fighting and I won't
Fight anymore to keep going.

5-15-16
g.r.j

Constant

One, *pound.*
Two, *pound.*
There's this constant pain I feel every day.

Three, *pound.*
Four, *pound.*
Consistent looks I get,
Frequent comments that people always make.

Five, *pound.*
Six, *pound.*
Will life get easier or will it always remain
The same?
How much longer can I take this
Constant ache I feel,
As I constantly break,
Day after day?

5-16-16

g.r.j

Care

Are you okay?
How are you doing?
Do you know how often I get asked that question?
Too often
Do you honestly care how I am?
If you did, would you treat me better?
Would you leave me for "more important things"?
People generally don't care about how you are
Because if people honestly did, they would treat you
better.

5-24-16
g.r.j

It's Like a Bruise

Depression is like a bruise that never goes away
A bruise in your mind
You just got to be careful not to touch it where it hurts
It's always there, though
I'm tired, in pain and have actually been really
depressed lately
I can't sleep because I'm constantly fighting with my
thoughts and in physical pain
While you're falling asleep,
I'm crying
While your dreaming,
I'm contemplating whether or not to hurt myself more
It seems to get worse at night and all I can do is
continue to fight
I'm tired of fighting for things that hurt me and
constantly struggling to keep myself together
I don't mean to shut down when I get like this and I
hope you don't take it the wrong way
When you are always struggling you start to feel numb
from your surroundings

8-21-16
g.r.j

Mental Health Resources

- **Mental Health – Sickle Cell Consortium**
- **Counseling & Support — Sickle Cell Disease Foundation (scdfc.org)**
- **oneSCDvoice | join our Sickle Cell Community**
- **Sickle Cell Support Groups and Organizations (sparksicklecellchange.com)**
- **Lifeline (988lifeline.org)**
- **NIMH » Help for Mental Illnesses (nih.gov)**
- **Home (veteranscrisisline.net)**
- **Tools and Resources (cdc.gov)**

Maybe That's Just Me

When you look in the mirror do you like what you see?
Your eyes might have bags under them
Cheeks that might have too much fat in them than you
would like
Wrinkle lines that weren't there but have made a
home on your face because of the constant worries of
everyday life
The reflection you see resembles just the outside that
will continue to change over time
What the reflection doesn't show you in the mirror is
what really matters
Your experiences that have shaped your thoughts and
realities
Maybe that's just me.

10-8-16
g.r.j

I'm usually depressed for no reason
or in an episode.

G.R.J

What's The Matter?

You know how you ask me "what's the matter?" and I
tend to say nothing?
That's because it's easier to say nothing at all than try
to explain something that I don't Even understand.
The voices in my head,
The need to isolate
And the urge to cry every time something happens.
I'm usually depressed for no reason or
In an episode.
Triggered by the smallest things
And when I get like this, people tend to take it
personally like I don't want to talk or don't Enjoy their
company.
I personally don't enjoy myself.

12-31-16
g.r.j

Endlessly Cycle

Do you ever just feel like you can't breathe?
Like you're being suffocated from within?
I've been feeling like this for more than several days.
It sucks.
To see others around you breathing air,
As if it's nothing,
While you're barely holding on to life.
Looking in, people probably think you're one of them.
That your lungs fill with air and exhale just the same
as theirs.
But only those suffering can truly see that you haven't
been able to breathe for years.
An endless cycle that has yet to be broken
Has become your life.

2-6-17
g.r.j

The Darkness

When the sun isn't out that's when it's the worst.
There's no glimmer of hope to hold on to anymore.
Your body is drained from putting on a mask all day
around people who don't Understand or either hiding
themselves.
Your thoughts get louder as the sun sinks back under
the horizon and there's nothing You can do.
Loved ones around you sleep peacefully at night while
you wrestlc with your thoughts in the ring.
Time seems to stop as you slowly start to lose yourself
within the darkness.
Eventually, the darkness consumes you until the sun
comes up.
You dread day after day, until one day you don't see
the sun anymore.

3-19-17
g.r.j

Bang

Words can hurt more than physical pain
When those around you don't understand,
When tension is high,
Your mouth can be the last resort to tearing someone
down
They can load a gun with their thoughts and feelings,
Pulling back the trigger,
Aiming for your heart
Bang!
Within seconds, you're bleeding
Wounded,
Trying to mend the damage
That someone you love caused
Bleeding out on the floor
The thoughts and pain
Flow from where the gun wound entered
Directly into your heart
No air to breath,
No room to forgive
Closing your eyes to the deception
From the person who knows you all too well
Standing behind the gun

3-26-17
g.r.j

Big Brown Eyes

Light brown hair,
Big brown eyes
A smile that is contagious and you will never forget
Time stopped whenever I was in your presence
It was as if you were the only thing I could see
A puzzle piece that I couldn't figure out, but never
gave up on
Something that was new and exciting at the same time
You hold a secret from those who are closest to you
Something that has always been who you are, but fear
holds it from truly showing itself
The most beautiful things tend to go unseen, but you
are different
A beauty that can't be replicated, but only dreamed
about
Hiding a part of you is like not being noticed at all
I hope that one day you relieve yourself from this
secret you try so hard to hide
Because I want to see all of your beauty

3-26-17
g.r.j

Foreign Concept

I tend to remember the bad things more often than
the good.
I think it's hard to think about the good when half of
your life has been the complete Opposite.
The numerous amounts of negative things that impact
you tend to decrease your Chances of truly being
happy
Your mind starts to not even register the good things
that happencd because they are a foreign concept

4-1-17
g.r.j

What is Love?

How do you when you love someone?
Love should take your breath away
Love is something that cannot be defined just by one
person
It's different for everyone which is why it's so hard to
find
You know you're in love when you feel as though
You can't live without that person
It's hard to breathe when you're not in their presence,
And your love for that person is so deep, it actually
begins to hurt
For some people love isn't that hard to figure out
Growing up, we are taught how to love one another
But when you are not truly taught what love is,
Can you still be loved?
If all the relationships you look up to have failed in the
end
Is it possible for you to find something that won't?

4-2-17
g.r.j

Suffocating

Some days it is hard to breathe let alone walk
How do you walk when you no longer have nowhere
to go?
How are you supposed to smile when there is nothing
that brings you happiness?
Pain is something that is not unfamiliar to me
I live with it; I struggle with it and sometimes it
consumes me
My body aches for an escape while my mind is
trapped in a continuous cycle of defeat
I have yet to find a way to be pain-free, and maybe
there isn't

4-30-17
g.r.j

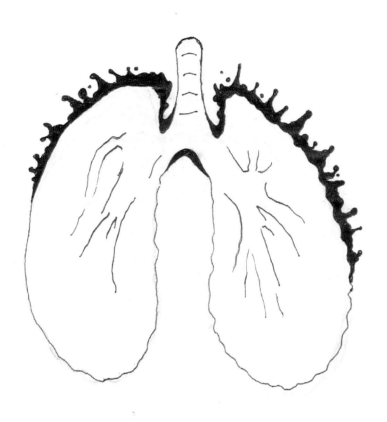

I lose myself in my thoughts, and relationships, but most of all in my pain

G.R.J

Control

Control is something that is an idea rather than
something that is realistic.
It is rare that you have complete control of your life
I lost control a long time ago
It started when I realized I couldn't control those that
meant the most to me
People tend to have a strong effect on me which can
sometimes be a problem
I don't think I've ever had control of myself and if I
have, it had always been very little
I lose myself in my thoughts, relationships, but most
of all in my pain
I've always remembered being in pain
It's something that I carry around with me every day
and have yet to get rid of.

5-16-17
g.r.j

Communication

Communication is something that is broken in this generation.
We use apps to pursue
Relationships
And
Hookups.
We text instead of talking on the phone.
When faced with a situation where communicating with someone in person is necessary, people are unaware of what we should do.

6-15-17
g.r.j

Virtual Reality

Sitting in a movie looking at a screen...
Not the one that's in my lap but the one in front of me.
I look to my left then to the right,
I see people not seeing me,
We're all caught in our lives
That had become a virtual reality,
From the devices that are slowly controlling our
dreams.

11-24-17
g.r.j

Reassurance

When it seems as if the world is crashing down on
you,
When you are past your breaking point and there is
nothing left to give:
There are things that go unnoticed that people in pain
tend to do
They give reassurance to those around them
Whether it is a fake smile, hug, or small talk that
you're not interested in
They don't want those around them to feel what
you're feeling
or even get a glimpse of it
Because they don't want to be seen as weak or
someone who is just seeking attention

6-18-17
g.r.j

Damaged

Am I hard to love?
My past defines me.
I struggle with the present
And the future is something that is always unclear.
I'm not as healthy as I can be.
Born into an illness that sometimes controls me.
A family that hasn't always been the best.
Ripped apart from my parents before I could even walk.
I had no chance.
School was a place I could thrive, but my peers rarely included me, so most of the time I isolated.
The hospital is a place I know too well.
Poked and scanned, I feel less like a human and more like an experiment every time I visit.
How could somebody love me when all I am is a damaged product of my environment?

6-29-17
g.r.j

High

It's been more than a year
Since I've felt that kind of high
The vulnerability of being so close to someone yet the anticipation of wanting more
Once you have partaken in this full-body sensation it
Unlocks a part of your mind that can linger these desirable thoughts—
Sometimes without control
I wonder if it's because we were created to experience this intoxicating moment with someone or it's actually a sin
If you think about what you want too much, your body will start to react
Hands will start to appear on your body as if they were made to be there
Your arms will start to tingle as the goosebumps appear
Thoughts start to intensify and the moment you've been waiting for is just on the horizon with an arch of the back
A soft whimper
You know you've tasted the high you've been craving for all to long

1-12-18
g.r.j

Confused

If you were concrete in how you feel about me,
The feeling you get when you are with me and us
There would be no confusion
What you're telling me wouldn't matter
Wanting to move forward with me would be easy
Your fear of getting hurt or experiencing any type of
pain would outweigh all your thoughts of being with
me
The fact that you are confused, shows me that you
don't know what you feel toward me
You have yet to realize what you have in front of you
and you still have a lot to figure out

1-14-18
g.r.j

Pain demands to be felt.

G.R.J

When People First Meet Me

I've been told that I'm not someone who is easy to
figure out.
I think this is because I'm not really sure myself.
I've experienced a lot of things at such a young age.
I'm really just trying to piece everything together.
When people first meet me,
I hope they feel
the pain behind my eyes,
the scars that I hide,
the tears that I have cried
and the things that I wish I could unsee.
Pain is something that demands to be felt.
Scars show your battle wounds to those around you.
Tears taste like salt because they feel just as bitter
when they are released
And our thoughts are what hold us captive from truly
being free.

2-20-18
g.r.j

Speechless

The best things in life are the things you least expect
Who would've thought that I would have met
someone as beautiful as you
I don't think there are many words to describe you,
but only one which is amazing
I love the way I feel when I am with you
You have yet to notice me and the way I look at you
I have yet to experience holding your hand, to feel the
presence of your warmth and the softness of your lips
I hope one day you feel the same way about me

2-21-18
g.r.j

When I Like Someone

There's this thing that happens
when I first meet someone, I like.
My thoughts start to scramble like eggs
Wow, she's beautiful.
My stomach turns with butterflies because I just
managed to make you laugh and I feel like I'm doing
something right.
Was that actually funny?
My voice tries to stay stable as I talk to you.
I want to hold your hand so badly right now.
My hands sweat as I walk with you close to me,
longing for it to be closer.
Should I kiss her?
As I take you home, I feel anxious knowing that it's
now or never.
Do you think she can tell I'm about to pass out?
My heart beats out of my chest as I slowly lean in.
Please don't pull away.
As my lips crash onto yours
Finally!
I knew that this moment was worth the wait.
There's this thing that happens
when I first meet someone, I like...

3-14-18
g.r.j

Permanently Gone

Spending time with you has its ups and downs
Just like any other relationship, right?
Constantly being in and out of each other's lives
makes me think about what it would be like if you
were permanently gone
You have never really lived up to the role model you
were supposed to be to me
Something that was supposed to be a continuous
loving and nurturing relationship
This has resulted in empty conversations and
meaningless interactions
Growing up I always hoped that you would turn into
something more than just a voice on the phone or a
figment of my imagination
Being older now I realize you were never ready for the
role you were supposed to be in my life

3-28-18
g.r.j

I Had a Dream

I dreamed about you last night
It was probably the best dream I have had in a while
I promise it's not what you think
I crave the most innocent parts of a relationship &
I finally held your hand in my dream
Something so simple
Made me the happiest person on the earth
Hopefully, I will work up the courage to do this soon
& be able to feel what I've been longing for

3-30-18

g.r.j

Invincible

Do you ever feel like you're invincible?
That in this moment nothing can stop you from
anything you want?
I feel this way sometimes, but it's hard to conserve.
The moment it happens- it's gone.
Comparing my happiness to tears and pain.
Constantly trying to overcome something that is a part
of me.
Experiencing pain without any warning.
Drawing the line between when to suffer or swallow
more pills...
All while trying to battle an underlying issue that
every pill, I take has a side effect

12-5-18
g.r.j

Yourself

I watch as you try to not break
As you start to repack your things into the suitcases
you have been living out of for over the past six
months
Trying to keep your composure
I slowly start to lose mine
I don't want you to see what I'm thinking
So, I make excuses for the way that we are treating
you
This feeling I'm experiencing is something
I never thought I would have to process so quickly
Having to take on the role
That you were always supposed to provide for me
Trapped and beaten by the mistakes you
Have chosen to make
Who knew that you would be drowning
In the hole, you dug yourself

12-30-18
g.r.j

Breathe

Breathe,
there's a sudden tightness in my chest.

Breathe,
searching for a clear mask,
clear liquid and a tube.

Breathe,
using the little energy, I have
to plug in a machine.

Breathe,
I put the mask over my head.

Breathe,
the feeling of medicine
slowly diffuses into my lungs.

Breathe.

12-31-18
g.r.j

Your Own Reflection

You are someone that I will always talk to
Yet I feel like the more we talk, the farther I am from
you
There is a distance that is growing between us
Things are less important and the connection we have
is slowly fading
I'm not sure if it's because you're afraid to let me truly
see who you are or that your Secrets are slowly
starting to consume you—
Not allowing you to recognize yourself while looking
at your own reflection
Trying to decide what's more important:
The mask you wear
Or
Being yourself

1-3-19
g.r.j

How Are You Feeling?

This is the million-dollar question I get asked quite
too often.
I guess you would expect that having a chronic illness,
right?
But the thing that really bothers me with this question
is how I'm *supposed* to answer it.
Society has trained us to be uncomfortable with the
truth and in its place be comfortable with pleasing
Others.
So, we say, "I'm fine" when we could be close to a
breakdown
Or
"I'm okay" because it's easier than explaining what we
are truly are feeling.
I'm tired of constantly experiencing this question that
I can't fully answer.
It's not that simple.
To completely answer it, it would take a whole
evaluation on my pain, thoughts, and emotions.
But who has the time for that?
So, I end with this final thought:
How are you feeling today?

1-11-19

g.r.j

What Will I Do?

I came into your life in a very unique way
Stories are told about how you were the first person to
hold me when I was born
Ever since then there has been a moment where we
are always in each other's corner
You are my rock and I am your paper
We make each other yet we are almost the same
I love the bond we have been able to create yet it
scares me at the same time
How will I live without you?
What will I do when you are gone?
These are the things I try to not think about as days go
by
Cherishing the moments, we have and encouraging
new experiences together

1-12-19
g.r.j

Happily, Ever After

I woke up crying this morning.
It wasn't because I had a bad dream.
My reality had reached a state of depression.
Sign after sign, love continues to fail me.
Whether it's a boy or a girl, nothing works
Is it because I have trouble loving myself?
Haunted by my past and constantly reminded of a
sickness I can't outrun.
Temporary enjoyment from romance in novels or
movies.
The hourglass for love is starting to run out.
Last call for Happily Ever After
Only looking to be held—
Be everything someone needs.
Will love conquer all or is it just a state of touch that
people are trapped in?

1-18-19
g.r.j

No Rewind Button

I was going to say "Hi"
Or you know... the nervous "Hey"
That literally everyone says when they first meet
someone but this isn't the first time
I have seen your face before,
Felt your lips on my skin,
Remember your laugh and the way your cheeks went
up corner to corner when you smiled
Yet the feeling of you standing in front of me is
different
We are different
Because there is no longer an us
No, it's not a You and I
It's just different
Because I can't unlove you
I can't erase the time that we spent
Because there's no rewind button in real life
Just play

6-6-19
g.r.j

Moments

Moments are things that you are supposed to hold
onto and cherish—
I feel trapped in mine
There are moments that don't feel real
Because they are too good to be true
These are the moments that I never want to end
Then there are the nights where I can't sleep
My back is screaming with agonizing pain that
radiates from within and I can't help but force tears
from my eyes
These are the moments that I wish never existed
Yet they last forever
This is my life and it continues
To hurt,
Break me down,
Push me past my breaking point,
Then hit repeat

6-11-19

g.r.j

Take a Shower

Take a shower
This was the first thing I was told to do
To cope with the urge of self-harm
The water
Sensation stimulates a different response
And changes your urges

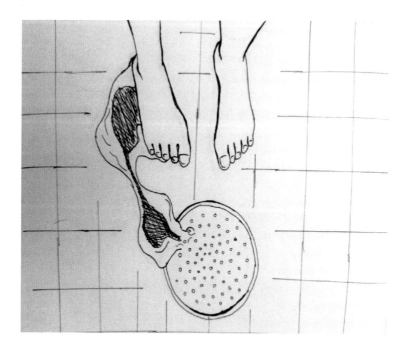

Depression presents itself in different ways
It is not a monster that hides under your bed
It's bolder
It hides within you
Knows all your secrets and tells you lies that make you
turn into a person you hate

How to destroy something that is intertwined with all the good and bad parts of you?
You learn how to tame your thoughts—
The beast within
Become stronger every day and you are able to turn down the voices

6-12-19
g.r.j

Unrealistic Reality

I can't stop crying
My body is aching
Sad from the events that are happening around me
One moment we are laughing and dining
Then with just a blink of the eye,
We are at each other's throats
I am only human
Yet sometimes I feel you don't see me
The pain I have
The way it controls my life
It's something you never want to think about
You load your gun with painful words that hit me
straight in the head than the heart,
Falling to the ground
I get a glimpse of a person I never thought I would see
When did you lose sight of the word family?
You are breaking our tree built with a generation of
names
Breaking like glass time after time
I can't stop crying
You were supposed to be there for me instead you
chose to back away
I'm not sure when the script changed, but I don't want
to be cast in your idea of how things should be
You are living in a selfish unrealistic reality

6-14-19
g.r.j

A Call

A call I was waiting for turned out to be
Not what I expected
Answering with a fully open mind,
Ready to hear nothing, but the good news
Yet within seconds, I knew that something was wrong
The tone of her voice said it all and once the words
were spoken,
They could not be ignored
Within an instance, all my hopes and dreams changed
From an altered reality to just simple pain
I didn't know what to say
What questions to ask
I just stood there, writing down the information that
was being spoken but meant nothing To me at that
moment
False hope is what I was fed
The taste was bitter
Maybe one day you will understand
What it feels like to have something you've been
waiting for
Taken away in the blink of an eye

6-21-19
g.r.j

Front Row Seat

Innocence, Love, And Happiness.
A bundle of joy
Climbs into your arms with thick eyelashes,
Big brown eyes and a smile
Instantly, holding your heart forever.
A love that you could only imagine
Is now in your presence.

Hope, Faith, Laughter.
She is smarter than we have yet to discover.
Inventing,
Observing all that is around,
Holding close those she loves
While sharing her heart,
With no doubt about anything she does.
Although her time on this earth hasn't been long,
There is so much life within her soul.
She is going to grow up to be something no one
Could ever fathom.
I'm just glad I have a front row seat to the show.

11-3-19
g.r.j

The Calm Before the Storm

Wind and air forming from the ground
No reason,
No explanation
Clouds cover the sky, allowing for darkness to
consume
Within seconds
You are swept up by the pieces that are your life
Spinning in past memories
Mistakes that you wish
You could take back
Yet continued to make one by one
Wedged between the perception of what you think
and reality
The tornado in my life
Coming at times when I least expect it
Deciding how big the destruction
As well as the path it will take
Then disappearing just as fast
It's exhausting to be trapped in a tornado zone
Fear of the unknown
Changing your plans during the calm before the storm

11-22-19
g.r.j

Know Your Worth

Tears run down the side of your cheek
I can see the fear in your eyes
You're tired of being hurt
The pain that the men cause,
The lies they tell you about yourself
Constantly you put yourself in these positions that I
still don't understand
I know you want more for yourself
A different life that you have yet to grasp
You have yet to change your destiny
Making endless mistakes based on your imperfections
and what you think you're worth
You're more than what you see
The lies are not true and the path is about to change
The door shuts and I'm closed off from the
destruction that continues to be your life
Let me in so I can see what you bottle up
Tell me your fears and your hopes
Let's dream together
No pain
No more tears
It's time to truly know our worth and start to heal our
wounds

11-17-19
g.r.j

The Undeniable

Hands raised,
Eyes closed
The undeniable ambiance
Knowing that your presence is always here
Worship your name with the breath given by your
lungs
Giving praise to a God that started life that is all
around
Speaking truth that is provided by your words
Teaching those who have become before and those to
come

12-29-19

g.r.j

Third Version of You

Lately, I feel like I know two different individuals
One that I'm familiar with
Putting on a smile
Always quick to jump on anything to please and give
to everyone else around you
Your alter ego is not someone I know right off the bat
They are quick to catch a temper
Say things without thinking
Don't have a good way of showing how they truly feel
All while making those around them feel less
appreciated and loved
I miss the third version of you
Where your eyes were always filled with hope
You could enter a room and instantly fill it with your
bright personality and bubbly walk
Fashion from head to toe is always on point
It was hard not to smile within your presence and feel
like you were the only person I knew

3-18-20
g.r.j

Missing You

I'm missing you tonight
The thoughts of us
Are vivid in my brain
Your smile,
Voice,
Personality
Inebriety within my veins
Trying to shake the love that is no longer a part of me.

4-10-20
g.r.j

See the Same as Me

You make me sick
Looking at you
Knowing that you are a fraud
Your name is not yours
Shouting,
Parading like you are something you're not
Ashamed of the past and running to scrape up a future
You make me sad for the way you live
The path you continue to forge
When will you set fire to a new light
Take the wheel of your destiny
Smarter than you think you are
Stronger than you look
History that has made you stronger
You could do anything you set your mind to and time
too
When will you see the same as me?

4-18-20
g.r.j

Sharing my Story

To shake hands of those who run an empire
To be in a room where the atmosphere is thick of
wealth and experience
To be able to meet and talk amongst those who have
started from the bottom and are now here
Being introduced
To walk onto an empty stage
Lit up for me and others to come
Sharing our story
Meeting celebrities
Thus, to be known as the Celebrity of the company
Being able to reach those without physically touching
them
Yet their hearts opened and motivated
For countless days to come and their line of work
This is what God has gifted me:
A voice and a platform

4-27-20
g.r.j

Tattoo

I crave your body and touch
Yet don't want the hurt and neglect
I want to feel you trace your lips up and down my
body
But don't want to be more than an item
I want you to hold me and rub my back as it hurts
However, I can't stand to look at you and remember
what you've done
You continue to cross my mind
Engraved like a tattoo
Something I can't erase but will try to forget

4-30-20
g.r.j

Make-Up

Putting on a shade that is lighter than my own
completion,
Under my eyes,
Neck and
Forehead
Every crevasse needs to be filled
To give a different
Subtle appearance
Applying multiple shades of colors
On various areas of my eyelids
To match my clothes but not overpower the look
Brushing my eyelashes up
In circular motions
Giving them definition
Completing the work that is done
Called makeup
Art
Men gawk at it
Others could care less
An industry solely based on looks and foundations

5-1-20
g.r.j

I'm Fine

Are you okay?
Yeah.
I'm fine.

5-6-20
g.r.j

Child Warfare

Brown curly hair,
Plump lips,
Colored eyes interlaced with her story,
Starts from the beginning
Two people in love
Lust,
Sex,
Pain,
A baby
The light of their world
Pride and joy
Hate and Bitterness
Takes the place of their love
Which is being ripped up
Day by day,
There's a child in this war of a divided house

7-7-20
g.r.j

Just a Photo

It's just a photo, right?
Looking at you
Then me
It's two different things
How did this distant
Empty Space,
Less than centimeters,
Became miles apart?
Hurt and lost,
I'm longing to belong
To just be
Live a simple life
Like the women do on tv

5-3-21
g.r.j

Girls

Girls, females,
women:
they make me nervous.
Not initially,
but intimately
I never know what to say
or what to do -
if I should hold her hand
or just be a friend.

Attractive females are my weakness,
working towards a common ground
is the first step
then I'm lost.
It's her body,
eyes, breast,
touch.

I will take charge of my gender,
women are too beautiful
to let them not know it.
It's time to experience her
inside and out,
kissing from up to down,
sucking the uncertainty
out, until
I can feel
the uncomfortable situation fades out.

8-2-21
g.r.j

The Sheets

Folding of the sheets
Packing and unpacking of bags
Multiple
Locations
Accounts
Slipping into the streets
With new men
Sleeping in rooms that don't belong to you
Trying to fill a void with the life you have created from
endless mistakes
Within the depth of who you are and the decisions
that continue to haunt you

11-15-21
g.r.j

The Grim Reaper

He was a sharp pain that never quite went away
but was there just to remind you
that he was never going to leave,
the sickle-shaped blood was the weapon of his choice
and in any instance, you would be at his mercy.

Darkness,
draining
your energy,
fading, pain
coming in waves,
weakness
in waning -
let go of me or will this be the death
of this person I used to be,
years and years of coming after me
with endless pain,
instances of near-defeat.

Who knew that Haploidentical

would be here to slay the one

they call the reaper

of Sickle Cell disease,

for no longer will my life

belong to them.

11-18-21

g.r.j

Thank You

Dear Reader

From the bottom of my heart, thank you for purchasing this book. It means a lot to be able to share with you my personal mental health journey and the relationships that affected them. I hope it helps you or someone that you may know. Please leave a review on Amazon and use the contact form to stay in touch with me (next page). I would love to hear your thoughts on the book, your favorite poem, or hear your personal story. I can't wait to hear from you. Look out for upcoming updates provided via my social media or my email list. Thank you!

Lots of love,
Genesis Jones

Contact Form

Made in the USA
Monee, IL
08 September 2023

41926495R00052